SMOKE AND MEAT

Complete Smoker Cookbook for Real Pitmasters
The Ultimate Guide for Smoking Meat, Fish, and Vegetables

DANIEL MURRAY

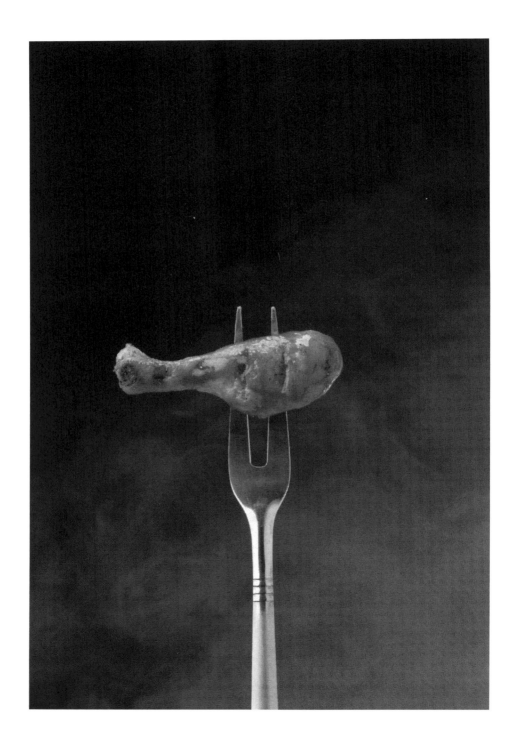

Table of Contents

AN INTRODUCTION TO SMOKED FOOD   6

BEEF RECIPES   7
SLOW COOKED SMOKED PORTERHOUSE BEEF STEAKS   7
SCRUMPTIOUS SMOKED BEEF BRISKET   10
LIP-SMACKING SMOKED BBQ BEEF CHUCKS   13
TASTY SMOKED RIBS GLAZED WITH BBQ AND HONEY SAUCE   16
SMOKED BEEF BODACIOUS BARBEQUE RIBS   19

POULTRY RECIPES   22
SMOKED TURKEY LEGS WITH CRISPY SKIN   22
WHOLE SMOKED TURKEY   25
FLAVORY TEA SMOKED WHOLE DUCK   28
TASTY WHOLE SMOKED CHICKEN   31
SMOKED BLOODY MARY WINGS   34
SMOKED CHICKEN LEGS   36

PORK RECIPES   39
SMOKED PULLED PORK   39
THE ULTIMATE SMOKED PORK BUTT   42
SWEET AND SAVOURY SMOKED PORK RIBS   47
JUICY GRILLED SMOKED PORK CHOPS   50
JUICY GRILLED SMOKED PORK   53

LAMB RECIPES   **56**

PERFECTLY COOKED SMOKED LAMB LEG   **56**
PERFECTLY COOKED SMOKED LAMB LEG   **59**
IRISH-STYLE SMOKED LAMB   **62**
GRILLED ROSEMARY LAMB CHOPS   **64**

FISH RECIPES   **67**

BRINE SMOKED FISH   **67**
AMAZING SMOKED FISH WITH GARLIC PARSLEY SAUCE   **69**
SMOKED SALMON FISH   **72**
GARLIC SMOKED SALMON FILLET   **75**
GARLIC SMOKED SALMON FILLET   **78**

VEGETABLE RECIPES   **81**

SMOKED GRILLED VEGETABLES   **81**
PERFECTLY SMOKED CORNS   **83**
ROASTED GARLIC POTATOES   **85**
SMOKED POTATOES WITH ONIONS AND GARLIC   **88**
SAVORY SMOKED ASPARAGUS   **91**

SMOKE AND MEAT   **93**

TYPES OF SMOKERS   **93**
ELECTRIC SMOKERS   93
GAS SMOKERS   93
CHARCOAL SMOKERS   94
PALLET SMOKERS   94
TYPES OF SMOKER WOODS   **95**
THE DIFFERENT TYPES OF CHARCOAL AND THEIR BENEFITS   **97**
LUMP CHARCOAL: 97
CHARCOAL BRIQUETTES: 97

THE DIFFERENCE BETWEEN BARBECUING A MEAT AND SMOKING IT?

98

BARBECUING MEAT: *98*

SMOKING MEAT: *99*

THE CORE DIFFERENCE BETWEEN COLD AND HOT SMOKING   **100**

THE CORE ELEMENTS OF SMOKING   **101**

THE BASIC PREPARATIONS FOR SMOKING MEAT   **102**

CHOOSING SMOKER   *102*

CHOOSING FUEL   *102*

TYPE OF SMOKING METHOD   *102*

SOAKING CHIPS OF WOOD   *102*

SET SMOKER   *103*

SELECTING MEAT FOR SMOKING   *103*

GETTING MEAT READY   *104*

PLACING MEAT INTO THE SMOKER   *104*

BASTING MEAT   *104*

CONCLUSION   **106**

GET YOUR FREE GIFT   **107**

AN INTRODUCTION TO SMOKED FOOD

Through history, smoking been a preferred way of preserving food, but it so much more than just a way to keep food from going bad! Smoking also introduces complex and delicious flavors into dishes that are otherwise often bland or uninteresting. In modern cooking, it's a great way to mix up staples in your home cooking, and it can be a really fantastic way to wow people at a potluck, or to host an incredible dinner party. Smoking is not only inventive and delicious, it also makes it really easy to make large quantities of food at the same time without too much fuss.

Traditionally, smoking is done by burning wood chips in a small enclosed area with the food, allowing the food to be cooked very slowly, while absorbing the rich smoky flavor. Today, smoking is often associated with sports tail gaiting parties and small family get-togethers. This guide is designed to both embrace that culture, and also offer up some techniques and recipes that will let you take your smoking to the next level: full blown gourmet food full of layered and nuanced deliciousness.

Beef Recipes

SLOW COOKED SMOKED PORTERHOUSE BEEF STEAKS

TOTAL COOKING TIME 3 HOURS

INGREDIENTS FOR 4 SERVINGS

THE MEAT

- 2 full-size porterhouse beef steaks – at least 1-1 ½ inch thick (2.5 lbs. each, 1.1 – kgs.)

THE RUB

- Black Pepper (freshly grounded)- 1 1/2 tablespoons
- Kosher Salt – 1 teaspoon

THE FIRE

- Outside Grill or Outside Smoker
- Wood chips (apple, hickory or mesquite)
- Charcoals

METHOD

1. Mix kosher salt and freshly ground black pepper in a small bowl.
2. Rub the steaks generously with the salt and pepper on each side.
3. Insert 3 – 4 metal skewers to secure the meat from falling off the grill.
4. Now light up 8-9 charcoals and place them inside the charcoal grill. Now add 2 – 3 chunks of wood chips and set the cooking grate in place.
5. Now place the steaks on the cooking grate.

6. Now cover the grill and arrange the top and bottom vents ¾ closed. Keep cooking and add 8-10 more coals underneath the grill until the temperature reaches around 170 - 210 °C or 338 – 410 °F.

7. Keep track of the internal meat temperature until it reaches 105-110°C or 221 – 230 °F to get medium-rare. If you want medium then let it cook for more 1 – 2 hours.

8. Now shift the steaks to the hotter side of the grill and let them cook for 45 seconds on each side

9. Now cover the steaks for another 45 seconds and let them quickly cook.

10. Open the lid and remove the steaks to the cutting board.

11. Carve and serve with mashed potatoes or grilled vegetables.

SCRUMPTIOUS SMOKED BEEF BRISKET

TOTAL COOKING TIME 6-7 HOURS

INGREDIENTS FOR 8-12 SERVINGS

THE MEAT

- Whole Packer Brisket (14-lbs - 6.3-kgs.)
- Beef Broth (1 ½ cup)

THE RUB

- Garlic Powder - 2 heaped tablespoons

- Paprika Powder - 2 tablespoons

- Onion Powder – 2 tablespoons

- Red Chili Powder – 2 tablespoons

- Black Pepper (grounded) – 1/3 cup

- Kosher Salt – 1/3 cup

THE FIRE

- Outdoor Smoker

- Applewood chips (2-lbs - 0.9 kgs)

METHOD

1. Take a medium bowl, add garlic powder, paprika powder, onion powder, red chilli powder, ground black pepper and kosher salt. Mix them well.

2. Now rub all the ingredients on the brisket well on all sides.

3. Let it aside for half an hour.

4. Prepare the outdoor smoker until it reaches a temperature of 225-230 °C or 437 – 446 °F.

5. Now place the brisket inside the smoker with fat side down

6. Now let it cook for 3-4 hours into the smoker until reaches the temperature of 160 °C or 320 °F (use a meat thermometer)

7. When it reaches the temperature of 160 °C or 320 °F remove it and double wrap it with a foil paper along with the beef broth.

8. Keep adding the Applewood to maintain the heat level.

9. Now again place the brisket inside the smoker and let it cook until it reaches the temperature of 205 °C or 401 °F (will take about 3 hours more)

10. Once done, remove it from the smoker grill, unwrap it and let it rest for 15-20mins.

11. Cut into slices and enjoy!

LIP-SMACKING SMOKED BBQ BEEF CHUCKS

TOTAL COOKING TIME 12 HOURS

INGREDIENTS FOR 8 – 10 SERVINGS

THE MEAT

- 1 Beef Chuck Roll (4-5 lbs., 1.8 – 2.2 kgs.)

THE RUB

- Black Pepper (grounded)- 1/3 cup

- Kosher Salt – ¼ cup

- Garlic Powder – 1 heaped tablespoon

THE FIRE

- Charcoal Grill
- Charcoal (3 lbs. 1.3 kgs)
- Wood chips

METHOD

1. Take a small bowl and mix kosher salt and ground black pepper.

2. Rub the mixture on the beef chuck roll properly

3. Now take a twine and tie the beef chuck roll around its circumference with an interval of 1 inch.

4. Prepare your charcoal grill, pour in the charcoal inside the grill. Once lit and have a grey layer of ash on them transfer half of them onto the charcoal grate. Set the cooking grate properly in place, cover the grill and preheat for at least 5 minutes.

5. Now place the beef chuck roll on the cooler side of the grill, cover it and let the beef get enough smoke

6. Add wood chips with the charcoal during cooking

7. Maintain the smoke until it reaches the temperature of 150 – 165 °C or 302 – 329 °F (about 3-4hours)

8. Now remove the beef chuck roll and wrap it with strong double foil and place it back on the grill and cover with lid. Let it slow cook for 4.5 – 5 hours.

9. Remove from the grill, and unwrap the foil. Let it rest for 30 minutes.

10. Cut the beef rolls into slices and discard the twine.

11. Serve with pickles, sliced onions or fresh garlic bread.

TASTY SMOKED RIBS GLAZED WITH BBQ AND HONEY SAUCE

TOTAL COOKING TIME 2.5-3 HOURS

INGREDIENTS FOR 2-3 SERVINGS

THE MEAT

- 2 Racks of Beef Ribs - around 8 bones on each rack (9- lbs - 4.- kgs.)

THE RUB

- Crushed Black Pepper - 1 teaspoon

- Kosher Salt - 1 tablespoon

- Sweet Paprika Powder – 3 heaped tablespoons

- Brown Sugar – ½ cup

- Garlic Powder – 2 teaspoons

- Onion Powder – 2 teaspoons

- Cinnamon Powder – 2 teaspoons

- Cayenne Powder – 1 teaspoon

- Dry Mustard Powder – 2 teaspoons

- Coriander Powder – 1 teaspoon

THE SAUCE

- Brown Sugar – 2 tablespoons

- BBQ Sauce – ½ cup

- Honey – 3 tablespoons

- Salt to taste

THE FIRE

- Outdoor Smoker or Charcoal Grill

- Soaked wood chips (3 lbs - 1.3 kgs)

- Dry wood chips (2 lbs - 0.9 kgs.)

METHOD

1. Take a small bowl and add all the dry ingredients; kosher salt, crushed black pepper, brown sugar, sweet paprika powder, garlic powder, onion powder, cinnamon powder, dry mustard powder, cayenne powder and coriander powder. Mix all the ingredients well.

2. Now rub this mixture evenly all over the ribs.

3. Place the marinated ribs into a tray and cover it. Let it rest in the refrigerator overnight.

4. Next day, take a small bowl and mix all the wet ingredients for the sauce; BBQ sauce, honey, brown sugar and salt. Set it aside.

5. Take out the ribs from the refrigerator and let them come to a room temperature. Preheat the grill to 104 °C or 220 °F

6. Use the wood chips to maintain the heat inside the smoker or grill.

7. On the grill, place the ribs and let them cook slowly for 2-3 hours with the closed lid

8. Brush the sauce over the rib racks properly after every 20-25mins

9. Ribs will be ready when the meat is tender and easily pull off the bones

10. Take out the ribs and let them rest for 20mins

11. Slice the ribs between bones and enjoy

SMOKED BEEF BODACIOUS BARBEQUE RIBS

TOTAL READY TIME 17 HOURS 30 MINUTES

TOTAL COOKING TIME 8 HOURS

INGREDIENTS FOR 10 SERVINGS

THE MEAT

- Beef Ribs (5-lbs - 2.3-kgs.)

THE RUB

- Paprika Powder - 2 tablespoons

- Cayenne Powder - 1 teaspoon

- Salt - 1 tablespoon

- Black Pepper (grounded) - 1 ½ teaspoons

- Onion Powder - 1 teaspoon

- Cumin Powder (grounded) - 1 teaspoon

- Brown Sugar - 1 ½ teaspoons

- Cinnamon Powder - 1/4 teaspoon

- Ground Cloves - 1/8 teaspoon

- Ground Nutmeg - 1/8 teaspoon

THE FIRE

- Outdoor Smoker

- Soaked hickory wooden chips (2-lbs - 0.9 kgs.)

METHOD

1. Take a large bowl, add paprika powder, cinnamon powder, ground black pepper, salt, ground nutmeg, cayenne powder, onion powder, cumin powder, ground cloves and brown sugar.

2. Mix all the ingredients well.

3. Apply evenly on the ribs, make sure that it covers all parts of the ribs.

4. Take a large roasting pan and place the ribs in it, cover it with foil paper and let it rest in the refrigerator overnight.

5. Remove the ribs from the refrigerator at least an hour before cooking.

6. Prepare the outdoor smoker at least for an hour until it reaches a temperature of 200 – 230 °C or 392 – 446 °F

7. Place the ribs into the smoker for good 6 to 8 hours

8. Make sure to add wood chips into the smoker after every 30-35 minutes to maintain a steady heat

9. Ribs will be done when you see a crispy thin layer on outer layer of the ribs and tender on the inside.

10. Remove the ribs from the smoker after the prescribed cooking time or when you see that they are done the cooking.

11. Let them rest for 10-15mins

12. Serve and enjoy the ribs

POULTRY RECIPES

SMOKED TURKEY LEGS WITH CRISPY SKIN

TOTAL COOKING TIME 35 MINUTES

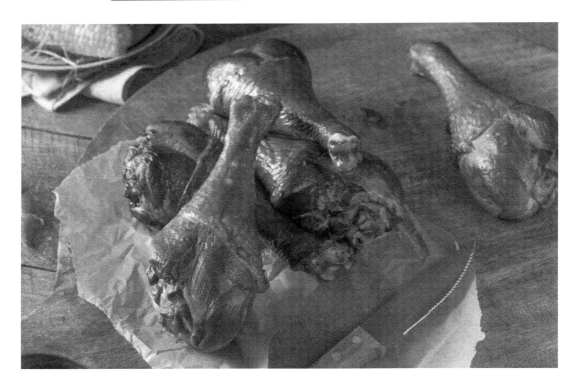

INGREDIENTS FOR 4 – 6 SERVINGS

THE MEAT

- 4 Turkey Legs with skin - (2.5 lbs - 1.1 kgs.)

THE MIXTURE

- Warm water – 1 gallon

- Cold water – ½ gallon

- Ice – 4 cups

- Barbeque Rub (Traeger) – 1 cup

- Curing salt – ½ cup

- Brown sugar – ½ cup

- Allspice berries (crushed) – optional – 1 tablespoon

- Black peppercorns (whole) – 1 tablespoon

- Bay leaves – 2 leaves

- Liquid Smoke – 2 tablespoon

THE FIRE

- Outdoor Smoker or Charcoal Grill

- Soaked wood chips (3 lbs - 1.3 kgs)

METHOD

1. Take a large stockpot and add one gallon of warm water, normal water, peppercorns, curing salt, BBQ rub, liquid smoke and 2 bay leaves.

2. Now bring the mixture to the boil until the salt is dissolved along with all spices.

3. Let it cool to room temperature.

4. Now add ice cubes and cold water, let it chill in the refrigerator. Now add the turkey legs to the prepared mixture and make sure that they are properly brined.

5. Let it sit for 24 hours, after that drain the turkey legs and pat dry with paper towel.

6. Prepare your grill with open lid for about 4-5 minutes and the fire is properly established. Now set the temperature to 250 °F or 121 °C with the lid closed for about 15 minutes.

7. Now place the turkey legs directly on the grill and smoke for about 4-5 minutes until the internal temperature of the meat reaches 165 °F or 74 °C. Check with a meat thermometer.

8. The turkey legs should look crispy brown on the outside and light pinkish from the inside.

9. Remove the turkey legs from the grill and serve hot.

WHOLE SMOKED TURKEY

TOTAL COOKING TIME 10 HOURS 20 MINUTES

INGREDIENTS FOR 13 SERVINGS

THE MEAT

- 1 Turkey (whole, without giblets and neck) - (10 lbs - 4.5 kgs.)

THE RUB

- Garlic cloves (crushed) – 4 cloves

- Seasoned salt – 2 tablespoons

THE FILL

- Butter – ½ cup

- Flavored cola – 1 can

- Apple (quartered) – 1 apple

- Onion (quartered) – 1 onion

- Garlic powder – 1 tablespoon

- Salt – 1 tablespoon

- Black pepper (freshly grounded) – 1 tablespoon

THE FIRE

- Outdoor Smoker

METHOD

1. Prepare the smoker at about 225 to 250 degrees °F or 110 to 120 degrees °C.

2. Rinse the turkey in cold water properly and pat dry with paper towel.

3. Now rub the crushed garlic cloves all side of the turkey along with salt, rub gently.

4. Place the turkey in the roasting pan.

5. Fill the turkey with apple, onion, butter, cola, black pepper, garlic powder and salt.

6. Cover loosely with aluminium foil.

7. Let it smoke for at about 225 to 250 degrees °F or 110 to 120 degrees °C. For approximately 10 hours. Or until the internal temperature of the meat reaches to 180 degrees °F or 80 degrees °C.

8. Make sure to baste the turkey every 5-6 minutes with the juices in the roasting pan.

9. Once cooked, serve it mashed potatoes and grilled vegetables.

FLAVORY TEA SMOKED WHOLE DUCK

TOTAL COOKING TIME 3 HOURS 10 MINUTES

INGREDIENTS FOR 8 - 10 SERVINGS

THE MEAT

- 1 Duck (preferably with broad meaty breasts) - (10 lbs - 4.5 kgs.)

THE MARINADE

- Ginger Root (large) – 1 piece

- Spring Onions – 1 bunch

28

- Cloves (grounded) – 1 tablespoon

- Cassia Cinnamon – 1 piece

- Red peppercorns (Sichuan) – 1 piece

- Honey – ½ cup

- Kosher salt – ¼ cup

- Black tea (Chinese) – 1 cup

- Water – to dip/cover the whole duck

- Seasoned salt – 2 tablespoons

THE BASTING

- Vegetable oil – ½ cup or as needed

THE FIRE

- Smoking Oven

- Camphor wood (1 lbs. 0.4 kgs. chunks or chips)

METHOD

1. Take a deep kitchen pot and mix all the ingredients in it with water, except the vegetable oil.

2. Now place the duck inside the bath mixture and refrigerate overnight.

3. On the next day, pat dry it properly and let it come to room temperature (2 hours).

4. Now hang the duck with the oven hook from the upper neck area.

5. Now take the camphor wood, brown sugar and tea bags and place them on a pan under the smoking oven's grill and set the temperature at about 350 degrees °F or 176 °C.

6. Let the duck roast for approximately 40 minutes (the timings also depend on your oven and size of the duck, so check accordingly)

7. To get a super crispy skin increase the temperature to 400 degrees °F or 204 °C in the last 10 – 15 minutes.

8. Baste the duck with vegetable oil in the last 10 – 15 minutes to get crispy skin.

9. Cut into slices and serve hot.

TASTY WHOLE SMOKED CHICKEN

TOTAL COOKING TIME 2.5 HOURS

INGREDIENTS FOR 4 – 6 SERVINGS

THE MEAT

- 1 whole chicken with skin - (3-5 lbs., 1.4-2.3 kgs.)

THE RUB

- Rub (Big Game) – 1 small bottle

- Garlic (minced) – 1 teaspoon

- Lemon – 1 piece

- Yellow onion – 1 piece

- Garlic cloves (whole) – 4 cloves

- Thyme sprigs – 4 pieces

THE BRINE

- Kosher salt – ½ cup

- Brown sugar – 1 cup

- Water – 1 gallon

THE FIRE

- Outdoor Smoker or Charcoal Grill

- Soaked wood chips (3 lbs 1.3 kgs.)

METHOD

1. Make brine mixture, add brown sugar and kosher salt into 1 gallon of water.

2. Once the brine is made, add chicken to it and let it refrigerate overnight. Make sure that the chicken is fully submerged inside the brine.

3. Prepare the smoker grill, with its lid open until the firs are established within 4-5 minutes. Now set the temperature at about 225 degrees °F or 107 degrees °C and preheat it for 10 -15 minutes with closed lid.

4. In the meantime, remove the chicken from the brine and pat dry with towel paper.

5. Rub the chicken with minced garlic and Big game rub.

6. Now fill the chicken with lemon, onion and thyme and tie the legs with kitchen twine.

7. Now place the chicken on the grill and let it cook for 2-3 hours or until when the internal temperature of the meat reaches 160 degrees °F or 71 degrees °C (check with an instant meat thermometer).

8. Remove it from the grill, slice and enjoy.

SMOKED BLOODY MARY WINGS

TOTAL COOKING TIME 1 HOUR

INGREDIENTS FOR 6 – 8 SERVINGS

THE MEAT

- Chicken wings with skins - (2 lbs., 0.9 kgs.)

THE RUB

- Bloody Mary Salt (Traegar) – 3 tablespoon

- Bloody Mary mix (Traegar) – 2 cups

The Fire

- Outdoor Smoker or Charcoal Grill

Method

1. Season the wings with salt properly.

2. Prepare the grill, turn it on smoke with open lid for 4-5 minutes or until you see fire establishing inside the grill. Now close the lid and set the temperature to 350 degrees °F or 176 degrees °C for 10-15 minutes.

3. Place the wings directly on the grill and let it cook for 30 minutes, turn the wings often to get a crispy skin on wings.

4. Now transfer the wings to the aluminum pan and add the smoked bloody mary mix and mix well until fully coated on the wings.

5. Cover the wings and place it back on the wings for another 30 minutes. Add a little bit of water if you see that the mixture is drying.

6. Transfer wings to the serving plate and serve hot.

SMOKED CHICKEN LEGS

TOTAL COOKING TIME 2 HOURS

INGREDIENTS FOR 4 – 6 SERVINGS

THE MEAT

- 8 Chicken legs with skins - (2 lbs., 0.9 kgs)

THE RUB

- Olive oil – 2 tablespoons

- Chilli powder – 1 tablespoon

- Brown sugar – 1 tablespoon

- Espresso (grounded) – ½ tablespoon

- Cumin (grounded) – ½ teaspoon

- Lime zest – 1 tablespoon

- Kosher salt – 1 tablespoon

- Black pepper (cracked) – ½ tablespoon

- Smokey Barbeque sauce – ½ cup

THE FIRE

- Outdoor Smoker or Charcoal Grill

METHOD

1. Take a small bowl and mix salt, black pepper, chilli powder, brown sugar, cumin, espresso and lime zest.

2. In a separate dish, massage the chicken legs properly with olive oil.

3. Now add the chicken legs to the rubbing mixture and coat well until the legs are fully coated with the dry mixture.

4. Cover the chicken legs and refrigerate overnight.

5. Prepare the smoker grill with open lid until the fire is established (takes about 4-5 minutes).

6. Now place the chicken legs on the grill and cook for 1 hour.

7. After 1 hour, increase the grill temperature at about 350 degrees °F or 176 degrees °C and cook for another 1 hour or until the internal temperature of the meat reaches 165 degrees °F or 73 degrees °C.

8. In the last 10 minutes of cooking, baste the chicken legs properly with barbeque sauce.

9. Remove from the grill and serve hot with fresh mint.

PORK RECIPES

SMOKED PULLED PORK

TOTAL COOKING TIME 20 HOURS 10 MINUTES

INGREDIENTS FOR 20 SERVINGS

THE MEAT

- 1 Pork Shoulder Roast Piece (8 lbs – 3.6 kgs.)
- Apple Cider – 1 quart or as required

THE RUB

- Plain white sugar – 5 tablespoons

- Brown Sugar (light) – 5 tablespoons

- Kosher Salt – 2 tablespoons

- Paprika Powder – 2 tablespoons

- Onion Powder – 1 tablespoons

- Garlic Powder – 1 tablespoons

- Black Pepper (freshly grounded) -1 tablespoons

- Onion (chopped) – 1 piece

THE FIRE

- Outside Smoker

- Wood chips (3 cups - hickory, apple etc.) soaked in water

METHOD

1. Take an extra-large pot and place pork inside it. Add a generous amount of apple cider to cover the pork.

2. Take a small bowl and mix together white sugar, brown sugar, kosher salt, black pepper, garlic powder, onion powder, and paprika powder.

3. Mix about a ¼ cup of the rub into the apple cider and reserve the remaining rub aside.

4. Now cover the pot with lid and refrigerate it for 12 hours.

5. Prepare the outside smoker to around 99 degrees °C or 210 degrees °F

6. Add enough wood chips into the smoker to maintain the required heat

7. Take the pork outside the pot and transfer it to the centre of the smoker.

8. Apply the reserved rub on the pork properly.

9. Into the water-pan of the outside smoker add the pork brine along with chopped onion and ¼ cup of the rub.

10. Let the pork cook inside the smoker for about 8 hours, until very soft and tender.

11. Transfer pork to the large dish and let it rest for 30 minutes

12. Shred and enjoy

THE ULTIMATE SMOKED PORK BUTT

TOTAL COOKING TIME 12 HOURS 45 MINUTES

INGREDIENTS FOR 6 - 8 SERVINGS

THE MEAT

- 1 Pork Butt (5 lbs – 2.3 kgs.)

THE MARINATE

- Apple Cider Vinegar – 2 cups

- Corn Oil – 1 cup

- Pineapple Concentrate – 1 cup

- Non-iodized Salt – ¼ cup

- Paprika Powder 1/8 cup

- Worcestershire sauce – 1/8 cup

- White Pepper – 1/8 cup

- 1 chicken cube (dissolve it in 2 tablespoons of water)

THE RUB

- Sugar – ¾ cup

- Salt – ½ cup

- Black Pepper (freshly grounded) – 1/3 cup

- Paprika Powder – ¼ cup

- Onion Powder – 1 tablespoon

- Garlic Powder – 1 tablespoon

- Chili Powder – 1 tablespoon

- Celery Salt – 1 tablespoon

- Hickory Salt – 1 tablespoon

- Cumin (grounded) – 1 teaspoon

- Sage (grounded) – 1 teaspoon

- Cayenne Powder – ¼ teaspoon

THE SAUCE

- Yellow Mustard – 2 tablespoons

- Honey – 1 tablespoon

THE FIRE

- Outside Smoker

- Charcoal for the smoker

- Wood chips (2-3 cups - hickory, apple etc.) soaked in water for at least 30 minutes

METHOD

1. Take all the marinating ingredients and whisk them well into a medium bowl.

2. Now take all the dry ingredients of the rub and mix them well into a small bowl.

3. Take a small bowl and mix the liquid ingredients of the sauce. Once done transfer it into a squeeze bottle.

4. Make sure to reserve around 1 cup of the marinade aside. This will be used while cooking the pork butt.

5. Take the pork butt and inject the marinade into the pork from different places.

6. Now put the injected pork butt inside a plastic bag and cover with the remaining marinade properly.

7. Let it marinate in the refrigerator for 6-8 hours.

8. After 6 – 8 hours, remove the pork butt from the plastic bag and use paper towels to pat dry it.

9. Now apply some of the sauce on each side of the butt and sprinkle the rub generously onto it.

10. Now prepare your smoker to about 225 to 250 degrees °F or 107 – 121 °C

11. Add the wood chips to lit the coal

12. Now place the pork on the smoker, make sure that you don't overcook it. Let it cook for 2 hours and baste the pork with the remaining marinade and put it back inside the smoker to cook for another 1 hour.

13. Take it out from the smoker, baste again and cook for another 1 hour. Repeat the process for one more time.

14. Now remove the pork butt from the smoker and wrap it inside a foil paper and set it back inside the smoker and cook until the internal temperature reaches 200 degrees °F or 93 °C

15. Now remove it from the smoker and let it rest for 15 – 20 minutes.

16. Slice or pull, enjoy the meal as you may like.

SWEET AND SAVOURY SMOKED PORK RIBS

TOTAL COOKING TIME 5 HOURS

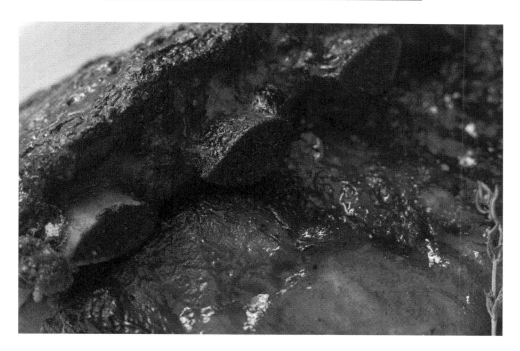

INGREDIENTS FOR 6-8 SERVINGS

THE MEAT

- 2 pork baby back ribs (10 lbs – 4.5 kgs.)

THE RUB

- Salt – ¼ cup

- White Sugar – ¼ cup

- Brown Sugar – 2 tablespoons

- Black Pepper (freshly grounded) -2 tablespoons

- White Paper (grounded) – 2 tablespoons

- Onion Powder – 2 tablespoons

- Garlic Powder – 1 tablespoon

- Chili Powder – 1 tablespoon

- Paprika (grounded) – 1 tablespoon

- Cumin (grounded) – 1 tablespoon

THE SAUCE

- Apple Juice – 1 cup

- Brown Sugar – ¼ cup

- Barbeque Sauce – ¼ cup

THE FIRE

- Outside Smoker

- Wood chips (3 cups - hickory, apple, peace etc. whichever you like) soaked in water for at least 35 – 40 minutes.

METHOD

1. Take a small bowl and add all the dry ingredients; salt, white sugar, brown sugar, black pepper, white pepper, onion powder,

garlic powder, chilli powder, paprika, and cumin together to make a dry mixture for the rub.

2. Now rub this mixture generously on both sides of the rib racks.

3. Wrap the marinated ribs inside a plastic wrap and refrigerate for at least 30 -35 minutes.

4. Prepare the smoker for about 270 degrees °F or 130 degrees °C), fill it with apple or hickory wood chips to maintain the heat and temperature.

5. Place the ribs racks inside the smoker and let it cook for 1 hour.

6. In the meantime, combine apple juice, brown sugar and BBQ sauce. Brush the ribs every 25-30 minutes with it after the first hour is completed.

7. Cook the ribs for about 3-4 hours more until it shrinks in size and the meat is no longer pinkish red.

8. Now brush the ribs with the remaining sauce 30 minutes before taking the ribs out of the smoker.

9. Once the ribs are cooked, wrap them tightly inside a foil and let it rest for 10 – 20 minutes.

10. Eat as it is or serve with mashed potatoes.

JUICY GRILLED SMOKED PORK CHOPS

TOTAL COOKING TIME 1 HOUR 30 MINUTES

INGREDIENTS FOR 4 SERVINGS

THE MEAT

- 4 Pork Rib Chops (centre-cut, ideally 1 ½ inch thick) (around 2 lbs – 0.9 kgs.)

THE RUB

- Kosher salt – as per taste

- Black Pepper (freshly grounded) – as per taste

THE FIRE

- Charcoal Grill

- Wood chips (2 cups - hickory, apple, peace etc. whichever you like) soaked in water for at least 35 – 40 minutes.

METHOD

1. Sprinkle salt on both sides of the pork chops and place them on a wire rack over a baking tray and let them rest in the refrigerator for at least 1 hour for up to 24 hours.

2. Now remove the pork chops from the refrigerator and sprinkle a good amount of black pepper and a bit of salt if needed.

3. Lit the chimney full of charcoal, when the charcoal is lit and grey out, take them out and place on one side of the charcoal grate. Set the grill properly and allow to heat up for 5 minutes.

4. Oil the grilling grate properly and place the chops on it until properly browned, ideally 3 -5 minutes per side.

5. Now move the pork chops on the cooler side of the grill with bone side up. Cover and let them cook until the internal temperature rises at about 135 °F or 57 °C.

6. Check with a meat thermometer.

7. Remove the pork chops from the grill and let it rest for 10 minutes before serving.

JUICY GRILLED SMOKED PORK

TOTAL COOKING TIME 1 HOUR 30 MINUTES

INGREDIENTS FOR 4 – 6 SERVINGS

THE MEAT

- 2 Pork shoulders roast, (8 lbs –3.6 kgs.)

THE RUB

- Brown sugar – ¼ cup

- White sugar – ½ cup

- Paprika powder – ½ cup

- Salt – 2 tablespoons

- Chilli powder – 1 tablespoons

- Cayenne powder – 1 teaspoon

- Black Pepper – 2 teaspoons

- Dried oregano – 1 teaspoon

- Cumin powder – 1 teaspoon

THE INJECTION LIQUID

- Apple juice – ¾ cup

- Water – 1 cup

- Sugar – ½ cup

- Salt – 3 tablespoons

- Worcestershire sauce – 2 tablespoons

THE FIRE

- Charcoal Grill or Outside Smoker

- Wood chips

Method

1. Mix all the dry ingredients into a bowl until well combined.

2. In a separate bowl, mix all the injection ingredients until the sugar and salt are well combined.

3. Inject each shoulder with the mixture with about ½ ounce per pound.

4. Now gently rub the dry ingredients mix on the pork shoulders properly.

5. Let it sit for 1 ½ hours at normal room temperature.

6. Place it inside the smoker, which should be set at a temperature of about 225 °F or 107 °C. Cook for 1 hour.

7. Remove from the smoker and let it rest for 5-10 minutes and serve fresh.

LAMB RECIPES

PERFECTLY COOKED SMOKED LAMB LEG

TOTAL COOKING TIME **14** HOURS

INGREDIENTS FOR **6-8** SERVINGS

THE MEAT

- Lamb leg (5-6 lbs - 2.2-2.7 kg.)

THE RUB

- Black Pepper (freshly grounded)- 1 teaspoon

- Sea salt – 1 teaspoon

- Dried Rosemary – 1 teaspoon

- Dried Marjoram – 1 teaspoon

- Wine vinegar – ½ cup

- White wine (dry) – ½ cup

- Olive oil – ½ cup

- Minced Garlic – 1 tablespoon

THE FIRE

- Outside Grill or Outside Smoker

- Wood chips or chunks (hickory), soaked for at least 30 -35 minutes.

METHOD

1. Mix together black pepper, salt, dried rosemary, dried marjoram, wine vinegar, white wine, olive oil and minced garlic in a small bowl.

2. Take a shallow dish and place lamb leg inside it, now pour the mixture on top of the lamb and cover it with lid and let it rest inside a refrigerator.

3. Prepare the smoker and let the coal and let it burn, now drain the wood chips and add it to the burning coals.

4. Take out the lamb from the tray, pour the remaining mixture into the water pan and place that water pan inside the smoker.

5. Now place the lamb leg at the centre of the smoker grill with close smoker lid.

6. Maintain the temperature of the smoker to about 225 °F or 107 °C.

7. Let the meat cook for 4 – 5 hours, or until the thickest portion of the meat's temperature reaches to 150°F or 65 °C

8. Maintain the temperature by adding charcoal, water and wood chunks as needed.

9. Now remove the lamb leg from the smoker and cover it tightly with foil and let it rest for 15 – 20 minutes

10. Slice and serve.

PERFECTLY COOKED SMOKED LAMB LEG

TOTAL COOKING TIME 6 HOURS 15 MINUTES

INGREDIENTS FOR 6 SERVINGS

THE MEAT

- 1 Medium size lamb shoulder (4 lbs - 2 kgs.)

THE RUB

- Brown sugar – 3 tablespoons

- Beer – ¼ cup

- Mint sauce – 1/4 cup

THE FIRE

- Outside Grill or Outside Smoker

- Wood chips or chunks (hickory or apple), soaked for at least 30 -35 minutes.

METHOD

1. Prepare the smoker until it reaches the temperature of 257 °F or 125 °C

2. Add a hand full of wood chips to maintain smoke inside the smoker.

3. Place the lamb shoulder inside the smoker and let it cook for about 3 hours.

4. Now remove the lamb shoulder and wrap it inside a foil paper with brown sugar and beer.

5. Place it back inside the smoker and let it cook for another 3 hours.

6. Should be cooked and the meat should start to lay off the bones easily.

7. Once cooked let it rest for 30 – 40 minutes.

8. Serve with mint sauce.

IRISH-STYLE SMOKED LAMB

INGREDIENTS FOR 6 - 8 SERVINGS

THE MEAT

- 1 Medium size lamb leg – without bone (4 lbs - 2 kgs.)

THE RUB

- Fresh Rosemary – 3 tablespoons

- Minced Garlic – 4 cloves

62

- Black pepper (crushed) – 2 tablespoons
- Kosher salt – 2 tablespoons

THE FIRE

- Outside Grill or Outside Smoker
- Wood chips or chunks (hickory or apple), soaked for at least 30 -35 minutes.

METHOD

1. Prepare the mixture for the lamb, mix all ingredients inside a small bowl.
2. Now properly rub half of the mixture inside the meat and the remaining on top of the meat.
3. Now tie the lamb leg properly with the kitchen twine thread.
4. Prepare the smoker and place the lamb leg inside the smoker. Let it smoke for about 4 hours at 225 °F or 110 °C
5. Remove the lamb leg from the smoker and let it rest for 30 -35 minutes.
6. Serve hot and enjoy.

GRILLED ROSEMARY LAMB CHOPS

TOTAL COOKING TIME 1 HOURS 20 MINUTES

INGREDIENTS FOR 4 SERVINGS

THE MEAT

- 12 lamb loin chops – at least 4cm thick (3.3 lbs - 1.5 kgs.)

THE RUB

- Fresh rosemary leaves (chopped) – 1/4 cup

- Minced garlic – 8 cloves

- Salt – 2 teaspoons

- Black pepper – 1 teaspoon

- Olive oil – 2 teaspoons

- Large rosemary sprigs – 8 pieces (soaked in water for at least 25 – 30 minutes)

THE FIRE

- Outside Grill or Outside Smoker

- Wood chips or chunks (hickory), soaked for at least 30 -35 minutes.

METHOD

1. Take a small bowl and add rosemary, garlic, salt, black pepper, and olive oil to make a thick paste.

2. Rub the paste on the chops properly on all sides. Let it rest for at least 15 minutes for up to 1.5 hours at room temperature.

3. Prepare the charcoal grill for cooking. Now put the rosemary sprigs directly on the charcoals.

4. Now as the rosemary sprigs begin to smoke place the lamb chops on the grill and cover it.

5. Turn the chops every 3-4 minutes each side.

6. Use the meat thermometer and check the temperature of the meat, remove it from the grill when it reaches the temperature of 130 °F or 54 °C

7. Remove from the grill and let it cool for 15 – 20 minutes

8. Enjoy the chops.

FISH RECIPES

BRINE SMOKED FISH

TOTAL COOKING TIME 6 HOURS 20 MINUTES

INGREDIENTS FOR 4 – 6 SERVINGS

THE MEAT

- 1 fish (any would work fine) - (5 lbs - 2.2 kgs.)

THE BRINE

- Water – 1 gallon

- Canning salt – 1 1/3 cup

- Brown sugar – 2/3 cup

THE FIRE

- Outdoor Smoker or Charcoal Grill

- Soaked wood chips – apple or hickory (2 lbs – 0.9 kgs.)

METHOD

1. Take a large stockpot and add water to it along with brown sugar and salt and mix well until sugar and salt are dissolved.

2. Now split the fish into two halves and dip them into the mixture. Refrigerate them overnight.

3. Prepare your smoker grill at about 180 degrees °F or 82°C and place the fish on the grill and cover the lid and let the fish cook for 3-4. Make sure to turn the fish while cooking.

4. Add wood chips to maintain the heat. Let the fish cook on slow smoke.

5. Once done, remove from the grill and serve hot.

AMAZING SMOKED FISH WITH GARLIC PARSLEY SAUCE

TOTAL COOKING TIME 2 HOURS 20 MINUTES

INGREDIENTS FOR 6 SERVINGS

THE MEAT

- 1 swordfish – 4 inch thick (without skin) - (4 lbs - 1.8 kgs.)

THE BRINE

- Kosher salt – 1 cup

- Sugar – 1 cup

- Black peppercorns – 2 tablespoons

- Water – 8 cups

THE RUB

- Canola oil – 3 tablespoons

- Salt – as per taste

- Black pepper – as per taste

THE SAUCE

- Canola oil – 2 tablespoons

- Garlic cloves (chopped) – 2 tablespoons

- Unsalted butter (cold) – 1 tablespoon

- Fresh parsley – 2 tablespoons

THE FIRE

- Outdoor Smoker or Charcoal Grill

- Soaked wood chips – Maplewood chips (2 lbs – 0.9kgs.)

METHOD

1. Take a large pot and add water, sugar, salt, peppercorns into it. Bring it to the boil until the sugar and salt are fully dissolved.

2. Let the temperature cool completely.

3. Now dip the swordfish into the brine, make sure it is fully submerged. Refrigerate it for overnight.

4. Prepare the outside smoker and set the temperature at about 220 – 250 degrees °F to 104 - 121°C.

5. Take the fish out of the brine and pat dry with kitchen paper towel and then let it air dry for another 1 hour at room temperature.

6. Now brush the fish with canola oil and sprinkle a pinch of salt and black pepper.

7. Place the fish on the grill and cook for 2 hours, keep adding the wood chips in the initial first hour to maintain the temperature.

8. Once cooked remove the fish from the grill and transfer to the platter.

9. For the sauce, add canola oil to the pan over medium heat and then add chopped garlic to it, stir for few seconds. Now add the butter stir for few seconds and turn off the heat.

10. Pour the sauce over the fish.

11. Serve hot and enjoy.

SMOKED SALMON FISH

TOTAL COOKING TIME 5 HOURS

INGREDIENTS FOR 4 SERVINGS

THE MEAT

- 2 large salmons fillets (without bones) - (4 lbs - 1.8 kgs.)

THE RUB

- Kosher salt – 1 cup

- Brown Sugar – ½ cup

- Black peppercorns (crushed) – 1 tablespoon

THE FIRE

- Outdoor Smoker or Charcoal Grill

- Soaked wood chips – apple or hickory (2 lbs – 0.9 kgs.)

METHOD

1. Take a large bowl and mix brown sugar, black peppercorns and salt.

2. Take aluminium foil and cut it a little larger than the size of the fish, coupled with an equally long cut plastic wrap sheet.

3. Now sprinkle 1/3 of the rub on the plastic and place the fish fillets on it with skins side down, now sprinkle the another 1/3 of the rub of the fleshy side of the fish.

4. Now cover the fish with the plastic wrap properly and strongly tie the aluminium foil from the edges.

5. Place the fish in a pan and cover with a lid and refrigerate for at least 12 hours.

6. After 12 hours, unwrap the fish and wash with water and pat dry with paper towel properly and let it dry on room temperature for 1-2 hours.

7. Prepare the smoker at 150 - 160 degrees °F or 65 - 71 °C and place the fish fillets on the grill and let it cook 1 – 1 1/5 hours or until the internal temperature of the thickest part of the fish reaches 150 degrees °F.

8. Remove from the grill and serve hot.

GARLIC SMOKED SALMON FILLET

TOTAL COOKING TIME 2 HOURS

INGREDIENTS FOR 4 SERVINGS

THE MEAT

- 1 large salmon fillet (without bones) - (2 lbs - 0.9 kgs.)

THE RUB

- Garlic cloves (minced) – 10 cloves

- Lemon juice – ¼ cup

- Butter – 3 tablespoons

- Sage (dried) – 1 teaspoon

- Oregano (dried) – 1 teaspoon

- Salt – ½ teaspoon

THE FIRE

- Outdoor Smoker or Charcoal Grill

METHOD

1. Prepare the outside smoker to smoker for 4 -5 hours at 200-225 degrees °F or 93-107 °C.

2. Properly wash and pat dry the salmon fillet.

3. In a separate bowl, take minced garlic cloves, lemon juice, butter, dried sage, dried oregano and salt.

4. Properly rub the mixture on the meaty side of the salmon fillet.

5. Now place the salmon fillet on the grill and let it cook on low heat for 2 hours (depends on the thickness of the fillet).

6. Check for the doneness after 1 hour.

7. Fish will be cooked when the internal temperature reaches 150 degrees °F or 65°C.

8. Remove from the grill and let the meat rest for 5-7 minutes.

9. Serve fresh with lime.

GARLIC SMOKED SALMON FILLET

TOTAL COOKING TIME 2 HOURS

INGREDIENTS FOR 6-8 SERVINGS

THE MEAT

- 6-8 catfish fillets - (4.5 lbs - 2 . kgs.)

THE BRINE

- Water – 8 cups
- Salt – 1 cup

THE RUB

- Cajun Seasoning – 1 pack
- Salt – as per taste
- Black pepper – as per taste

THE SAUCE

- Hot sauce – 1 cup

THE FIRE

- Outdoor Smoker or Charcoal Grill
- Wood chips – apple or peach wood chips (2 lbs – 0.9 kgs.)

METHOD

1. Take a medium size pot and fill it with water, add ½ cup salt to it and mix well. When the brine is ready to dip the fish inside the brine and refrigerates for at least 4 hours.

2. Prepare the smoker at about 200 degrees °F or 93°C.

3. Now take out the catfish from the refrigerator and remove from the brine and pat dry properly.

4. Sprinkle Cajun seasoning on the catfish fillets along with salt and pepper. Now drizzle some hot sauce on each fillet.

5. Place the catfish fillets inside the smoker and let them cook on low heat for 2 – 2 ½ hours, the fillets will absorb the smoke and you will get an amazing flavor.

6. Once you see that the skin has become flaky, especially the skin side. It's time to remove it from the smoker.

7. Let the catfish fillets rest for 10 minutes.

8. Serve hot.

VEGETABLE RECIPES

SMOKED GRILLED VEGETABLES

TOTAL COOKING TIME 45 MINUTES

INGREDIENTS FOR 4 SERVINGS

THE VEGETABLES

- 1 large Eggplant – sliced into ½ inch thick rounds slices

- 2 Bell peppers (red) – cut into halves and seeded

- 2 Bell peppers (yellow) – cut into halves and seeded

- 2 Zucchini – sliced ½ inch thick

- 2 Large red onions – peeled and sliced in ½ inch thick rounds

THE SAUCE

- Vegetable oil – 4 tablespoons

- Teriyaki sauce – 1 cup

THE FIRE

- Outdoor Smoker or Charcoal Grill

METHOD

1. Properly brush the vegetables with vegetable oil, apply oil on all sides.

2. Prepare the smoker at 200 degrees °F or 93 °C

3. Now place all the vegetables on the rack of the smoker in a single layer and smoke for about 30 minutes.

4. Now preheat the grill for about 4-5 minutes at 180 °F or 82 °C.

5. Brush the grate grill with oil, and arrange the vegetables on the grill and grill for at least 10 – 15 minutes turning once after 5 minutes.

6. Baste the vegetables with the teriyaki sauce every 4 minutes.

7. Remove the vegetables from the grill and serve with fresh lemon.

PERFECTLY SMOKED CORNS

TOTAL COOKING TIME 40 MINUTES

INGREDIENTS FOR 4 SERVINGS

THE VEGETABLES

- 8 fresh corns with husks

THE RUB

- Softened butter – ½ cup

- Fresh thyme (chopped) – 2 tablespoons

THE FIRE

- Outdoor Smoker or Charcoal Grill
- Wood chips – hickory or apple, soaked for at least 30 minutes (2 lbs –0.9 kgs.)

METHOD

1. Prepare the charcoal inside the grill, let the coals burn for 10-20 minutes.
2. Mix softened butter with thyme in a separate bowl.
3. Rub the butter mixture on the corns on all sides.
4. Pull the soft husks back to cover the corn and place it inside the smoker.
5. Let it cook for 30-40 minutes at about 180 °F or 82 °C.
6. Remove from the smoker and serve hot.

ROASTED GARLIC POTATOES

TOTAL COOKING TIME **1** HOUR

INGREDIENTS FOR **4** SERVINGS

THE VEGETABLES

- Small red potatoes (3 lbs - 1.3 kgs.)

THE RUB

- Olive oil – ¼ cup

- Kosher salt – 1 ½ teaspoon

- Black pepper (freshly grounded) – 1 teaspoon

- Minced garlic – 2 tablespoons

- Freshly chopped parsley – 2 tablespoons

THE FIRE

- Outdoor Smoker or Charcoal Grill

METHOD

1. Prepare the smoker grill at about 250 °F or 121 °C

2. Cut the potatoes into halves or quarter pieces.

3. Now take a medium bowl and add potatoes to it along with salt, black pepper and minced garlic. Toss it well until the potatoes are fully coated.

4. Take a sheet pan and transfer the coated potatoes to the pan and set them in one single layer.

5. Place the pan inside the smoker and let it cook for 45 minutes to 1 hour. Flip the potatoes every 15 minutes while cooking.

6. Cook the potatoes until crisp and golden brown.

7. Once cooked remove the potatoes from the smoker and toss with parsley.

8. Serve with cream sauce or salsa sauce.

SMOKED POTATOES WITH ONIONS AND GARLIC

TOTAL COOKING TIME 1 HOUR 10MINUTES

INGREDIENTS FOR 4 – 6 SERVINGS

THE VEGETABLES

- Fresh red skinned potatoes – quartered (2 lbs – 0.9 kgs.)
- 1 Large red onion – large chunks
- 5 Garlic cloves (crushed)

THE RUB

- Olive oil – 4 tablespoons
- Salt – 1 teaspoon
- Black pepper (freshly grounded) – 1/4 teaspoon
- Dried dill – 1/4 teaspoon
- Dried thyme – ¼ teaspoon
- Dried basil – ¼ teaspoon

THE FIRE

- Outdoor Smoker or Charcoal Grill

METHOD

1. Prepare the smoker at about 250 degrees °F or 121 °C.

2. Take a large baking tray or pan, place foil paper inside it and grease the foil with oil.

3. Take the vegetables in a large bowl and mix other ingredients in it, toss them well until the potatoes, garlic and onions are properly coated.

4. Set the vegetables inside the tray and place the tray inside the smoker. Let the vegetables cook for about 40-50 minutes, turning every 10 minutes.

5. Remove from the smoker when the vegetables are tender and crispy on the outside.

6. Let it sit for 10 minutes and serve with any sauce you like.

SAVORY SMOKED ASPARAGUS

TOTAL COOKING TIME 25 MINUTES

INGREDIENTS FOR 4 SERVINGS

THE VEGETABLES

- 1 bunch of Asparagus (thin spears)

THE RUB

- Olive oil – 3 tablespoons
- Sea salt – 1 teaspoon

- Black pepper (freshly grounded) – 1/2 teaspoon

- Lemon juice – 1 tablespoon

- Minced garlic – ½ teaspoon

- Parmesan cheese (grated) – 1 ½ teaspoon

THE FIRE

- Outdoor Smoker or Charcoal Grill

METHOD

1. Prepare the smoker at about 250 degrees °F or 121 °C.

2. Take a medium mixing bowl, add asparagus to it along with salt, black pepper, minced garlic, olive oil, and parmesan cheese and toss well.

3. Take a baking sheet with foil paper places inside the tray, place the asparagus in one single layer inside the tray.

4. Place the tray inside the smoker and let the asparagus cook for 10 – 15 minutes until tender.

5. Remove from the smoker when the vegetables are tender and crispy on the outside.

6. Squeeze lemon while serving and enjoy.

SMOKE AND MEAT

TYPES OF SMOKERS

ELECTRIC SMOKERS

The electric smoker is the best smoker because it is very simple to use. Just set it, put your food in it and leave rest of the work to the smoker. There is nothing an electric smoker can't grill, be it seafood, poultry, meat, cheese or bread. It requires little attention unlike other smokers like filling water bin, lighting wood or charcoal and checking on fuel frequently. Yes, unlike traditional smoker, electric smoker just need 2 to 4 ounce of wood chips that turns out a delicious and flavorful smoky food. Furthermore, they maintain cooking temperature really well. On the other hand, it sleek and stylish look and small size make it appropriate if you are living in apartment or condo. Due to their simpler functions and hassle-free cooking, the electric smoker is a good choice for beginner cooks who want to get started with smoking food.

GAS SMOKERS

Gas smokers or propane smoker are much like a gas grill using propane as a fuel. Therefore, the heat for cooking remains consistent and steady. Furthermore, gas smokers are as easy to use, just set the temperature and walk away. However, frequent checks need to be done to make sure fuel doesn't run out. It isn't a big issue but one should keep in mind. And the best part, a gas smoker can be used when there is no electricity or when you need an oven. A gas smoker can take up to cooking temperature to 450 degrees, making this smoker flexible to be used as an oven. Another fantastic feature of gas smoker is its portability so they can use anywhere. Just pack it and take it along with you on your camping trips or other outdoor adventures.

CHARCOAL SMOKERS

Nothing can beat the flavor charcoal gives to your food. Its best flavor just simply can't match with any other smoker flavor. Unfortunately, setting a charcoal smoker, tuning fuel, maintaining cooking temperature and checking food can be a pain and you might burn the food. Not to worry, these hassles of a charcoal smoker does go away with practice and experience. Therefore, a charcoal smoker suits perfectly for serious grillers and barbecue purist who want flavors.

PALLET SMOKERS

Pellet smokers are making a surge due to their best feature of a pallet of maintaining a consistent temperature. It contains an automated system to drop pallets which frees the cook to monitor fuel level. The addition of thermostat gives the user the complete control the cooking temperature and grilling of food under ideal condition. In addition, the smoking food uses the heat from hardwood which gives food a delicious flavor. The only downside of pallet smoker is their high cost between the ranges of $100 to %600.

TYPES OF SMOKER WOODS

Smoker wood is an important element which you need to decide correctly to cook a delicious smoked food. The reason is that smoker chips of woods impart different flavors on the food you are cooking in the smoker. Therefore, you should know which smoker wood should be used to create a delicious smoked food. Here is the lowdown of smoker woods and which food is best with them.

1- Alder: A lighter smoker wood with natural sweetness.
   Best to smoke: Any fish especially salmon, poultry and game birds.
2- Maple: This smoker wood has a mild and sweet flavor. In addition, its sweet smoke gives the food a dark appearance. For better flavor, use it as a combination with alder, apple or oak smoker woods.
   Best to smoke: Vegetables, cheese, and poultry.
3- Apple: A mild fruity flavor smoker wood with natural sweetness. When mixed with oak smoker wood, it gives a great flavor to food. Let food smoke for several hours as the smoke takes a while to permeate the food with the flavors.
   Best to smoke: Poultry, beef, pork, lamb, and seafood.
4- Cherry: This smoker wood is an all-purpose fruity flavor wood for any type of meat. Its smoke gives the food a rich, mahogany color. Try smoking by mixing it with alder, oak, pecan and hickory smoker wood.
   Best to smoke: Chicken, turkey, ham, pork, and beef.
5- Oak: Oakwood gives a medium flavor to food which is stronger compared to apple wood and cherry wood and lighter compared to hickory. This versatile smoker wood works well blended with hickory, apple, and cherry woods.
   Best to smoke: Sausages, brisket, and lamb.
6- Peach and Pear: Both smoker woods are similar to each other. They give food a subtle light and fruity flavor with the addition of natural sweetness.
   Best to smoke: Poultry, pork and game birds.
7- Hickory: Hickory wood infuses a strong sweet and bacon flavor into the food, especially meat cuts. Don't over smoke with this wood as it can turn the taste of food bitter.

Best to smoke: Red meat, poultry, pork shoulder, ribs.

8- Pecan: This sweet smoker wood lends the food a rich and nutty flavor. Use it with Mesquite wood to balance its sweetness.

Best to smoke: Poultry, pork.

9- Walnut: This strong flavored smoker wood is often used as a mixing wood due to its slightly bitter flavor. Use walnut wood with lighter smoke woods like pecan wood or apple wood.

Best to smoke: Red meat and game birds.

10- Grape: Grape wood chips give a sweet berry flavor to food. It's best to use these wood chips with apple wood chips.

Best to smoke: Poultry

11- Mulberry: Mulberry wood chips is similar to apple wood chips. It adds natural sweetness and gives berry finish to the food.

Best to smoke: Ham and Chicken.

12- Mesquite: Mesquite wood chips flavor is earthy and slightly harsh and bitter. It burns fast and strongly hot. Therefore, don't use it for longer grilling.

Best to smoke: Red meat, dark meat.

THE DIFFERENT TYPES OF CHARCOAL AND THEIR BENEFITS

Charcoal is one of the efficient fuels for smoking. It burns hot, with more concentrated fire. Smoking food with charcoal is awesome. Though lighting charcoals, regulating airflows and controlling the heat is always a challenge, however, the excellent taste of food is worth this challenge. But, keep in mind that not all charcoals are equal and selecting one is a matter of preference.

LUMP CHARCOAL:

Lump charcoal or hardwood is the first choice of griller as a better fuel source. It is basically made by burning wood logs in an underground pit for a few days. As a result, water, sap, and other substances in log burn out, leaving behind a pure char or lump charcoal. This charcoal burns pure, hot and efficiently. They burn hotter in the beginner and burn cooler by the end. Therefore, lump charcoal is a good choice for broiling quickly or searing food at intense heat. In addition, the lump char also add the aroma of wood smoke into the food which takes the taste to another level of gastronomical heaven. Since, lump charcoal cool its fire in 30 minutes, replenish fire to maintain the temperature which takes only 5 to 10 minutes by adding few unlit coals. It's recommended to use lump charcoal with a combination of wood chips like maple, oak or hickory and refuel this wood chips every 40 minutes during smoking food.

CHARCOAL BRIQUETTES:

Charcoal briquettes are actually crushed charcoal. The major benefit of using this natural charcoal is its even shape and size. This is done by adding chemical binders and fillers like coal dust and compressing into a pillow shape. Therefore, creating a bed of coals is very easy with charcoal briquettes which are quite hard with uneven and irregular charcoals. The only downside is that they burn very quickly, more than lump charcoal. This creates a short window for smoking food, therefore, more briquettes need to add during grilling.

THE DIFFERENCE BETWEEN BARBECUING A MEAT AND SMOKING IT?

There are two main ways to cook meat that has become an increasingly popular cooking method: smoking or barbecuing. They are both different and require different cooking equipment, temperature, and timing. Following is the full comparison between smoking and barbecue.

BARBECUING MEAT:

Barbecue is a slow cooking, indirectly over low heat between 200 to 250 degrees F. Therefore, it is best suited for beef brisket, whole pig, turkeys or pork shoulder. These animals tend to have tough muscles which need slow cooking over low heat to get a moist and tender meat. It turns out an extremely tender and flavorful meat. The best example of a perfect barbecue is falling of meat off the bones. During the barbecue, the fuel needs to be filled frequently but do this quickly, as lifting lid of burner exposes meat to air which can turn it dry.

For barbecuing meat, the grill needs to be preheated until hot. For this light enough charcoals or bкisquettes so that their fire turns down for cooking. In the meantime, season meat and then when grill reaches to perfect cooking temperature, place seasoned meat on it. Having grill on perfect temperature is essential as meat won't stick to grilling grate.

Equipment: Fire pit, grill or a charcoal burner with lid.

Fueling: Lump wood charcoal, charcoal briquettes or wood chips combination like apple. Cherry and oak wood chips.

Best to smoke: A big cut of meats like Briskets, whole chicken, sausages, jerky, pork, and ribs.

Temperature: 190 to 300 degrees F

Timing: 2 hours to a day long.

SMOKING MEAT:

Smoking is one of the oldest cooking technique dating back to the first people living in caves. It was traditionally a food preservation method and with the time, its popularity never died. Smoking is a related process of barbecue. It's the best cooking method to bring out the rich and deep flavor of meat that tastes heavenly when meat is smoked until it comes off the bone.

During smoking, food is cooked below 200 degrees F cooking temperature. Therefore, smoking food requires a lot of time and patience. It infuses woody flavor into the meat and turns a silky and fall-of-bone meat. There are three ways to smoke food, cold smoke, hot smoke and adding liquid smoke. In these three types of smoking methods, liquid smoke is becoming increasingly common. Its main advantage is that smoke flavor is controlled. In addition, the effect of liquid smoke on meat is immediate.

There is another smoking method which called water smoking. It uses water smoker which is specifically designed to incorporate water in the smoking process. The water helps in controlling the temperature of smoker which is great for large cut meats for long hours.

Equipment: A closed container or high-tech smoker.

Fueling: The container will need an external source for a smoke. Wood chips are burn to add smoky flavor to the meat. However, the frequent check should be made to monitor and adjust temperature for smoking.

Best to smoke: A big cut of meats like Briskets, whole chicken, pork, and ribs.

Temperature: 68 to 176 degrees F

Timing: 1 hour to 2 weeks

THE CORE DIFFERENCE BETWEEN COLD AND HOT SMOKING

There are two ways to smoke meat that is cold smoking and hot smoking. In cold smoking, meat is cooked between 68 to 86 degrees F until smoked but moist. It is a good choice to smoke meat like chicken breast, steak, beef, pork chops, salmon, and cheese. The cold smoking concern with adding flavor to the meat rather than cooking. Therefore, when the meat is cold smoked, it should be cured, baked or steamed before serving.

On the other hand, hot smoking cooks the meat completely, in addition, to enhance its flavor. Therefore, meat should be a cook until its internal temperature is between 126 to 176 degrees F. Don't let meat temperature reach 185 degrees F as at this temperature, meat shrinks or buckles. Large meat cuts like brisket, ham, ribs and pulled pork turns out great when hot smoked.

THE CORE ELEMENTS OF SMOKING

There are six essential elements of smoking.

1- Wood chips: Chip of woods are used as a fuel either alone or in combination with charcoals. In addition, these chips add fantastic flavor to the meat. Therefore, chips of wood should only be used which suits best to the meat.

2- Smoker: There are basically four choices from which a smoker should be the pick. The choices are an electric smoker, charcoal smoker, gas smoker and pellet smoker. Each has its own advantages and downsides.

3- Smoking time: Smoking time is essential for perfect of meat cuts. It is actually the time when the internal temperature reaches its desired values. It may take 2 hours up to more than two weeks.

4- Meat: The star of the show is meat that needs to be more tender, juicy and flavorful after smoking. Make sure, the meat you sure has fat trimmed from it. In addition, it should complement the wood of chips.

5- Rub: Rubs, mixture or salt and spices, add sweetness and heat to the meat. They should be prepared in such a way that all types of flavor should be balanced in the meat.

6- Mops: Mops or liquid is often used during smoking meat. It adds a little bit flavor to the meat and maintains tenderness and moisture throughout the smoking process.

THE BASIC PREPARATIONS FOR SMOKING MEAT

CHOOSING SMOKER

The major and foremost step is to choose a smoker. You can invest in any type of the smoker: charcoal smoker, gas smoker or an electric smoker. A charcoal smoker runs for a long time and maintain steadier heat in the smoker and give meat pure flavors. A good choice for beginner cook for smoking meat is a gas smoker where there is no need to monitor temperature but it comes with a downside that meat won't have much flavor compared to charcoal. On the other hand, the simplest, easiest and popular smoker is an electric smoker. Cooking with electric smoker involves only two-step: turn it on, put meat in it and walk away. Read more details about smokers in the section "type of smokers".

CHOOSING FUEL

Wood chips add a unique flavor to the meat, therefore, select that wood chips that would enhance the taste of meat. Some wood of chips have a stronger flavor, some have mild while others are just enough to be alone for smoking. Check out the section titled "types of smoker wood" to get to know and decide chips of wood that will complement your meat.

TYPE OF SMOKING METHOD

You have two choices to smoke meat, either using wet smoking, dry smoking, liquid smoke or water smoking. Read the section "The core difference between cold and hot smoking" to find out differences between each. In addition, go through smoking meat portion in the section "the difference between barbecuing a meat and smoking it".

SOAKING CHIPS OF WOOD

Wood chips need to soak in order to last longer for fueling smoking. The reason is dry wood that burns quickly and this means, adding fuel to the smoker which can result in dry smoked meat. There isn't any need of using wood chips when smoking for a shorter time. Prepare wood chips by soaking them in water for at least 4 hours before starting smoking. Then drain chips and wrap and seal them in an aluminium foil. Use toothpick or fork for poking holes into the wood chips bag.

SET SMOKER

Each type of smoker have its own way to start smoking. For wood or charcoal smoker, first, light up half of the charcoals and wait until their flame goes down. Then add remaining charcoal and wood chips if using. Wait they are lighted and giving heat completely, then push charcoal aside and place meat on the other side of grilling grate. This is done to make sure that meat is indirectly smoked over low heat. Continue adding charcoal and/or soaked wood chips into the smoker.

For gas/propane or electric smoker, just turn it on according to manufacturer guideline and then add soaked wood chips into chip holder and fill water receptacle if a smoker has one. Either make use of the incorporated thermostat or buy your own to monitor the internal temperature of the smoker. When smoker reaches to desired preheated temperature, add meat to it.

SELECTING MEAT FOR SMOKING

Choose the type of meat which tastes good with a smoky flavor. Following meat goes well for smoking.

Beef: ribs, brisket and corned beef.

Pork: spare ribs, roast, shoulder, and ham.

Poultry: whole chicken, whole turkey, and big game hens.

Seafood: Salmon, scallops, trout, and lobster.

GETTING MEAT READY

Prepare meat according to the recipe. Sometimes meat is cured, marinated or simply seasoned with the rub. These preparation methods ensure smoked meat turn out flavorful, tender and extremely juicy.

Brine is a solution to treating poultry, pork or ham. It involves dissolving brine ingredients in water poured into a huge container and then adding meat to it. Then let soak for at least 8 hours and after that, rinse it well and pat dry before you begin smoking.

Marinate treat beef or briskets and add flavors to it. It's better to make deep cuts in meat to let marinate ingredients deep into it. Drain meat or smoke it straightaway.

Rubs are commonly used to treat beef, poultry or ribs. They are actually a combination of salt and many spices, rubbed generously all over the meat. Then the meat is left to rest for at least 2 hours or more before smoking it.

Before smoking meat, make sure it is at room temperature. This ensures meat is cooked evenly and reach its internal temperature at the end of smoking time.

PLACING MEAT INTO THE SMOKER

Don't place the meat directly over heat into the smoker because the main purpose of smoking is cooking meat at low temperature. Set aside your fuel on one side of the smoker and place meat on the other side and let cook.

Smoking time: The smoking time of meat depends on the internal temperature. For this, use a meat thermometer and insert it into the thickest part of the meat. The smoking time also varies with the size of meat. Check recipes to determine the exact smoking time for the meat.

BASTING MEAT

Some recipes call for brushing meat with thin solutions, sauces or marinade. This step not only makes meat better in taste, it also helps to maintain moisture in meat through the smoking process. Read recipe to check out if basting is necessary.

Taking out meat: When the meat reaches its desired internal temperature, remove it from the smoker. Generally, poultry should be removed from smoker when its internal temperature reaches to 165 degrees F. For ground meats, ham, and pork, the internal temperature should be 160 degrees F. 145 degrees F is the internal temperature for chops, roast, and steaks.

CONCLUSION

As you can see from these recipes, the world of smoking is only as limited as your imagination! Sweet, savory, vegetable, mineral, meat- you can smoke almost anything. As you get more comfortable with these recipes, feel free to start experimenting on your own. The basic principles hold true, but your own taste buds can drive you. Good luck, and happy smoking!

GET YOUR FREE GIFT

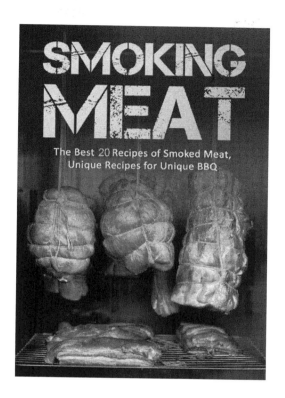

Subscribe to our Mail List and get your FREE copy of the book

'Smoking Meat: The Best 20 Recipes of Smoked Meat, Unique Recipes for Unique BBQ'

https://tiny.cc/smoke20